Encounters

Nadine K. Thompson

Encounters

First Edition: 2020

ISBN: 9781524315757
ISBN eBook: 9781524315856

© of the text:
   Nadine K. Thompson

© Layout, design and production of this edition: 2020 EBL Books

All rights reserved. No part of this publication may be reproduced, distributed, or transmitted in any form or by any means, including photocopying, recording, or other electronic or mechanical methods, without the prior written permission of the Publisher.

"Encounters" is a compilation of poems about daily life encounters and the psychological and social effects that they have on the individual. Encounters can be delicate and personal, fulfilling and happy, as well as subtle and sexy, and always with a hint of pain and heartbreak.

My name is Nadine Karen Thompson, and I am originally from Jamaica. I am an ESL teacher working in China, where I am also a member of the Hangzhou Writer's Association. I enjoy writing and sharing my poems. I have met many interesting people and encountered various situations. I hope you will feel and appreciate the journey as you read my poems.

Writing with appreciation and enthusiasm,
Writing from different points of views,
Writing as I view aspects of life,
Writing to feel the passion of life,
Writing as my mind relaxes,
Writing about nothing and everything,
Writing as my heart overflows,
Writing as a voice softly speaks over an intercom,
Writing to say everything,
Writing to explain and proclaim!

Japan for J.E.T.S

The JET Program,
Like a young mother,
Nurturing thousands,
Echoing their gurgling sounds.

This journey encapsulates,
A place of movement,
Caressing the footfalls of those who came and went,
Trekking through the 'inaka' and the city,

This magazine,
A receptacle of memories,
Of laughter, dreams, frustrations and fears.
These images would flood riverbanks.

This home video affirming,
An album of subtle sounds,
Capturing the faint whoosh of those who left,
The vibrations of those who are still here,
The rising anxiety of those who are yet to come.

This experience of exchange,
A lasting monument locked up in time,
Recording our histories,
Celebrating our victories,
Sealing our alliances,
Creating new perspectives,
Linking our destinies.

My travels

In all the places, I have been,
I have seen glimpses of me,
Of what the world is and what it might be.

Like London,
A city exciting,
Its rhythms subtly swell, you have to listen well,
Connecting with family,
Finding various flavors,
A melting pot of communities.

Like Cambridge,
A city of collective learning,
Engrafted in universities,
Punting through the seasons,
Admiring King's College,
Exploring bookshops and thrift shops,
Knowing the backs of Cambridge through parks and green spaces.

Like Kyoto,
Its history swells,
And captures the sound of the Japanese koto,
Reverberating through time and space,
A geisha makeover of beauty and aesthetics,
Framed with the backdrop of Kinkakuji.

Like Kobe,
Its colors blend and link a host of nationalities,
Oishii takoyaki, Kobe beef and kiwi chu-hai,
Street foods and summer festivals
Tech streets and Kobe harbor,
Its sound the music of fusion created by diversification.

Like Paris,
Its pomp and pageantry, affording you only a taste,
The Eiffel Tower tall and glorious,
Cruising along the Seine,
The pious yet friendly Mont Marche,
The music--the sound of French—
 brash, sassy and arrogant.

Like Monaco,
The suggestive and wild at heart,
Full of riches,
Able to caress you and mesmerize you.
Its music— the sounds of F150s.

Like Nice,
Nice, delectable, laying under the golden sun,
Charming and charmed by sun, fun and sea,
Diving into sweet passions,
Savoring a piece of heaven, Living the dream.

Like Rome,
Its music the sound of Italian chatter and romantic interludes,
The appetite filled with pizza and pasta,
The Colosseum impressive,
Reeling with great history, the past living in the present.

Like Frankfurt,
Its greenery through calm and serenity,
The music the sounds of transportation and the River Main,
Of interesting museums and apple wine,
A mecca of high- rise banks juxtaposing distinct architecture.

Like Seoul,
Its colors lively, bold and spicy,
The taste of kimchi and Korean barbeques,
Tantalizing and strong,
The underlying sights and sounds,
A tribute to a life that is fast moving.

Like Thailand,
Its warm smiles enchanting me
The sights and sounds of street food lingering,
The music, sounds of chatter and bargaining in markets,
Showing wisdom in simplicity and Thai massages.

Like Amami Oshima, Japan
Its hues natural as the first dawning,
The music, the sounds of birds and the sea,
The people sharing their everyday words of sincerity,
A place treasured as home,
Values, calm and enduring
Untouched by worldly excitement.
A world heritage for us all.

The Grand Canal

You're as long as you're wide.
I look out at the wide expanse as I walk along;
This side of the bridge.
Every morning,
Every evening,
I watch the cargo boats.
Driving by,
Some two,
Sometimes three.
I see you in the winter,
In the spring.
With character,
You carry on!

I take a stroll on the river boat,
Relaxing my mind,
Clearing my thoughts.
In a bottle of aromatic oils,
I take in the view.

I select a time of peace,
To let go of stress.
Start the day afresh.
In every walk,
I traverse along the Grand Canal.

Uneven pavements

On every street side,
The sidewalk
The footpath in China,
Uneven pavements
Reside and scatter,
Heels clicking in,
Heels clicking out,
A sloppy step,
Seesaw sliding up and down,
A splash here,
A gulp there, Unexpected force.
Unforeseen.
Trapping big feet,
Small feet,
Medium feet,
A sudden response to your quickened steps.
A break in your lost thought.
A reminder of your once twisted ankle
Wondering how it catches you off guard
At every inch, every turn.

My life in equations.
Walking on uneven pavements in China.
Every occasion a new feeling,
Unwilling to capture, Still remaining.
Not new, not old, A feeling,
When uneven.
Walking on uneven pavements.

Replacing the known cobblestone.
My life in parallel,
Crossing over,
Over paths
Moving through.
Forwards.
Backwards.
Walking on uneven pavements.

Navigating Ruins

Navigating an idea,
Awesome and gruesome.
Navigating through art, poetry and song.
Feeling abandoned in routine,
The unkempt gardens of our daily lives.
Telling stories lost and forgotten,
Putting the pieces together.
A navigator,
A seafarer,
An explorer.
Navigating time.

Convergence

Two waterways converged in my life,
The Grand Canal and the River Cam, Cambridge,
Converged in loss;
Loss of faith,
Loss of love,
Loss of newness of life.
Converged in sickness,
Suffering tremendously,
Feeling mediocre.
Converged in pain,
Reaching the rock bottom of the soul's spirit.
Nature converged to help me find healing
Urging me to stand in victory again.
Surrender to forgiveness and love,
Accepting where pain took me.
Looking out at the boats, the bridges and the gardens growing nearby, A new journey of self-discovery begins...

Landscape 1:

Jamaica

Small farm, crops growing, the village fed.
Ferns, growing wild, soon to die of weeds.
Small flower pots, enchanting flowers, makeshift garden.
House for warm weather, workmen chipping away, tiles laid.
Smells of fried fish, Mama's cooking, home style brew.
Dog and bird sounds, living in a village, baby asleep.
Peas, rising up in our garden, pick them in the pod.
Clothes on the line, neighbors conversing, and stories passed on.
Dandelions, swaying in the wind, a flower petal picked and blown.
Small country road, taxi hailing by, passengers alight.
Peas, now harvesting, soup for dinner.
Chopped firewood, cooking over outside fires, love in action.

Landscape 2:

Cambridge

Calm river, walking along the nearby park, tired body and mind.
Beautiful green space, creating tender footpaths, gives me peace.
Cobblestones on the street, clicking heels sounding, time cleverly trapped.
Purple flower garden, neatly hedging in, Botanical garden setting.
Neat houses, polishing brick walls with chimneys, church and bookstores crammed in the middle.

Landscape 3:

China

Typical apartment building, capturing city landscapes and movement, a home created.
Unlike a village, juxtaposing working people, schools and offices, the new China.
Prominent building, community leading, a school.
A player, navigating compromise, an enigma
The Canal, strolling by after work, peace sought.

ENCOUNTERS WITH A
MYRIAD OF FEELINGS

Half- Wit

Half -asleep, half- awake,
eyes half-closed, half-conscious,
half-heartedly I get out of bed,
in the half-light I walk halfway to the kitchen,
look at my half-finished dinner
and wonder why lately many things have been half-done.
I turn the radio on and listen to some half-truths
as the singer croons and I find that in this decision I'm half and half.
I pick up the phone and for half-a sec
I think I might call you then I realize
that this is the gift that we gave half -each to one another.
So, I eat half of my half- baked dinner
and return to bed half- starved, half-dazed and half-witted,
knowing that you were my better half.

Left to Chance

Things left up to chance are a chance and a half,
A chance gotten,
A chance taken,
A chance sought,
A chance lost.
A chance garnered,
A chance brokered,
A chance hoped for,
A chance in a deal break,
A chance in a chance,
A chance on a chance,
A chance left to chance,
A chance planned to a tee,
A chance with special ingredients,
A chance of unlimited potpourri,
The chances of you,
The chances of me,
A single line in unison,
Like two full breasts,
Teased into satisfaction,
What are the chances of that?

Transient Roles

Men are transient in the nature of their minds,
A cave man stuck in a cycle of transitioning,
Assuming roles,
Being assigned roles,
Fulfilling roles,
Relinquishing roles,
Competing in roles,
Marketing roles,
Symbolizing roles,
Carving out roles,
Abdicating roles,
Adjudicating roles,
Trapped in roles,
A straggler on a street-side,
Cashing in on mind games,
The temperature in passing remains,
Un-checked,
Un-avoided,
Un-supervised,
Un-authorized.

Mellowing

Mellowing;
Into a flow of energy.
Life, though spinning its roller coaster wheels,
Has us mellowing,
Into a glass of fine red wine.
Gently rolling along,
A nature ride held by captivating mountains,
And breathtaking blue hills,
Mellowing into different colors of shades of pink, blue, red and yellow,
Comfortable to be teased and laughed at,
Able to show pet peeves,
Shouldering criticism lovingly,
Asking questions un-coercively,
In a softness of fur,
That chooses forgiveness over anger.
Mellowing like a cast spell,
Into time zones and days and nights,
Into friendship wearing a coat of happiness,
Into decision-making becoming satisfied,
Into work blossoming into listless play,
A comedy of pin balls,
Mellowing into life, Into you,
A holiday spent caressing
Labels of contentment.

Mellowing,
Into rhyme and reason,
Rest and sleep,
Interacting and intersecting in steam and cold air,
Breathing in fresh air.
Mellowing into upside down and right side up,
A safe place to land,
A passenger not alighting.
An honest passion,
Holding us in a jar of sweets.
Mellowing like fall leaves,
Rich in color,
A smorgasbord of chocolate and fruits.
Mellowing through our taste buds and senses,
Mellowing into the people we've become.

Seeds

Seeds sown germinate
Their spurt unclear.
Unkempt fields of rocks and thorns,
Desert lands dry as chip
Cradle seeds in barrenness.
Seeds grow, blossoming, flowering, spreading,
Struggling against unknown forces.
Growth trapped within,
Resisting the forceful choke of death.
Thriving under duress,
Gaining strength under trampling feet,
Surviving harrowing conditions,
Persisting in darkness,
Capturing light,
Strengthening in the night,
Breaking forth at dawn,
Taking root above the earth,
Glowing with a life of its own,
Caressing the wind,
Bending its movement upwards and downwards.
A seed innately powerful
Unimaginable, how it grows.

Beginning and End

Alpha and Omega,
From start to finish
There is a thought
It lingers
Hanging on
A deep feeling
Frequent questioning
Pride and ego
Rivalry and Comradery
A testing of wills
Uniquely intertwined
Protective of the link
Listed under confidential
A revealing never to witness
Rushing along though cruising
Winding roads transfusing
A jump start
A slam of the brakes
Both capturing existence
Beginning and end
End and beginning.

Precedence

My love,
That which has taken precedence,
Has taken precedence.
In the wide ocean
Our times have tempered their courses,
Coursing through our veins,
A film reel of shots now stands,
A photo exhibition,
Cast in dim light,
Capturing silhouettes,
In different hues.
A chronicle of a feast of passion,
Interlocking joy.
We redesigned the decor,
Of a simple home,
In colors of dreams,
With unsaid pieces of art,
Joined through ripples of clothing,
Enhanced by the chiming of times,
Resonating in movement,
Sealed in a time capsule,
Love rising and slowing,
Lust burning and dying,
The unveiling,
Of our hearts' desires,
Transfixing and transposing,

Holding us together,
Trapping us in,
Keeping us back.
My love,
The essence of the beauty,
Of our times:
Waits and wades,
Waddling and twisting,
Vines growing on trees.
We got to the beach,
Felt the warm sunshine,
Relaxed in leisure,
A time to look back,
Show soulmates intertwining,
Firmly established in fulfilment.
My love,
Love fell into us.
Unexpectedly,
N sync,
Poetic, Dramatic,
Unhinging:
Beautiful and satisfying,
A waltz infused with salsa rhythm,
A dance of settled minds.

Seasons of You

My love
I have tried to love you both.
You are each a part of my journey,
In you I find beauty,
Frozen on lakes,
A coldness borne by,
Mittens and scarves,
Jackets and boots,
Wrapped up and covered under duck feather quilts,
Snuggles in bed and home cooked delights,
Clearly defines you,
Each year I am happy to be with you for a few wintry days,
Gray skies hang over us when you tarry,
Leaving me sad and flu bitten.

My other love comes strolling in,
Bringing sweet smelling buds,
Flowers of beautiful bright colors,
A walk in the park,
Chirping of birds,
Throwing off layers,
Planting seeds,
Of light heartedness,
A flourishing of the spirit.

I grew accustomed to having you around this time,
The wind is blowing a change,
New ships set to sail.
Go gently my winter love,
Rest well!
See you at the chiming of the clocks pushed back.
My other love is coming in robust radiance,
Quicken your steps now!
For the springtime harvest, Of our love garden.

Detaching

An itch to scratch,
Grows on creepers,
Eyeing too closely,
Monopolizing time,
Interfering,
Scrutinizing,
Possessive,
Proving inconvenient,
Bossy,
The chosen one,
Still on the waiting list,
Itching for the promise,
Scratching to stop the itch,
In a life of a wannabe,
Wrapped in fairytales,
Happy ever after,
I see.

Encounters

First meeting,
A sighting,
Seeing you,
Even if the traffic is congested.
A capturing
Of features
Eyes, smiles, movement.
A glance,
A spark tinkering the attention.
Not wanting to lose such a testament of attraction at first viewing.
A ripple of emotions coursing through.
Excitement!
Needing to see the target again.
The soul expanding,
The swelling up of the veins
The heart boiling over
Won't rest till it claims the prize.

Standing in a standstill

In speaking...
We have said nothing to each other
Tiptoeing around through hush tones,
Whispering on cue,
Silence. Deafening.
So loud in my ear, I whimper,
What do you really want to say?

In song through poetic form,
A heart on the sleeve,
You have needs to be met too.
Is it erotic denial or shame?
Keeping yourself contained in your cage,
But failed!
Will desire consume us?
Can it be enough?
We've opened a can of worms.
"Things break", she said.
It's all she could do to push you away.
What is the push factor or pull factor?

We've come to the middle of the road,
A journey leading to where,
Do you know?
We keep ourselves guessing.
Guessing!
Is it a possible alignment?
Stars beautifully appearing,
Sun and moon,
Under the shadow of an eclipse.

Hearts near a wishing well

If hearts when their wishing, wells
Swelled, press forward and took a breath,
Of air to keep itself from racing too fast,
Out of breath, out of time.
If hearts could hold back from conceiving,
What they're really wanting; you on a platter
You in full glory no matter the contrived scenarios of the best
or the worst.
If hearts could run away from themselves,
Hide behind doors and curtains and unsaid words,
Hearts would stop feeling and try philosophizing,
The times, the dates, the touch, the dealings.
If hearts could really tell, they would say,
Love doesn't want to be loving you in this way.

The Hammer

The silence of the morning broken,
Here it comes,
Thud, Thud, Thud.
The hammer head bounces off the nail on to the wall,
The building vibrates and shrieks,
Then in rhythmic chant the carpenter starts again,
Gong, Gong, Gong.
Like a band hyped up,
The tempo up-beat,
Clank, Clank, Clank.
The walls now screaming.
The veins in my head pulsating,
Like an earthquake the room spins,
Zoom, Zoom, Zoom.
In my head the drum beats
Ta dam, Ta dam, Ta dum, Ta dum.
My lungs burst forth and I wail,
Waah, Waah, Woah, Woah.
Like a baby disturbed too early in its sleep.

What is Love?

It's unassuming,
Yet bold,
It's as crazy as the waves on a stormy sea,
Yet calm like the wind after a storm.
It's as Oriental as the East,
 It's as Supreme as the West,
It's as prickly as thorns,
It's as soft as bamboo leaves,
It's as strong as the oxen,
It's as weak as the kitten,
It's as cunning as the fox,
It's as full of goodness as the dove.
It's as spirited as the horse,
It's as faint hearted as the mouse,
It's like a three minutes advertisement,
It's like a two-hour drama,
It's like the icing on a cake,
It's like the secret ingredient in a Christmas pudding.
It's like a garden full of flowers,
It's like the land when drought takes over,
It's everything and nothing,
It's up and down,
It's horizontal, it's vertical,
It's failure, It's success,
It's summer, it's winter,
It's today and it's yesterday,
 It's love and it's a mystery.

Romance with Words

Dream-like,
The waves kissed the shores,
Two hands interlocked,
The horizons peeping out,
Witnessed the mid-day scene,
Two pairs of feet gently brushed against the warm sand,
The wind hugging them.

The rocks opened their arms calling them,
To sit for a while.
In the thrill of the moment,
With currents running high,
Their touch a flood of electricity,
Like eagles they soared to the sky.
The wind released euphoria,
The air swooned with the scent of sweet perfume,
The day captured the voices,
Careful to record the promises.

The lonely sand crab filled with wonder,
Stopped to contemplate the aura,
The trees all around claimed freedom,
Each pebble grabbed a taste of life.

Eyes held tenderness requited,
The pull of heartstrings enchanted,
Dreams alive with wings a-lighted,
Hearts intertwined invited,
The hush of life,
Sublime and unabated.

Symmetry

I see shadows of you,
You see shadows of me,
Radiating clearly,
Vividly!
Like the other half of an orange,
Life's got symmetry.
My vision burns with clarity,
Your lens trapped the reality.
Like colors radiating in a prism,
Our focus glued like magnetism,
Eyes unaccustomed,
Precision lacking, See…
Dim light, Images blurry,
The shadows missing.

ENCOUNTERS WITH SPIRITUAL/POSITIVE LIGHT

Buds Opening

Buds opening,
Freshness,
Growth,
Sunshine,
Laughter,
Love,
Brightness,
Radiance,
Cheer,
Clarity,
Spring,
Bloom!
Let there be light!

First of June

Opening up like a bud,
Rising up to the sun,
Stretching forth,
Bending to the light,
Folding into beauty,
Becoming a rose,
Gathering scent,
Coloring the view,
Touching a life,
Giving a smile,
Realizing a dream,
Capturing a heart,
Releasing love!

Life

Enjoy it!
Live it!
Feel it!
Breathe it!
Inhale it!
Take it in!
Smell it!
Touch it!
Visualize it!
Contextualize it!
Accept it!
Endure it!
Hold on to it!
Release it!
Cherish it!
Nourish it!
Appease it!
Worry not about it!
Life,
Taste it!
Life,
Savor it!

I am a woman rising

I am a woman rising,
Rising from disappointment,
Rising from loss,
Rising from despair,
Rising from unbelief,
Rising from emptiness,
Rising from negativity,
Rising from fear,
I am a woman rising up!

I am a woman accepting blessings,
I am a woman finding happiness,
I am a woman experiencing hope,
I am a woman filled with abundance,
I am a woman abounding in positive light,
I am a woman rising higher and higher!

ENCOUNTER WITH
LOVE AND LOSS

Lily Cups

The world will not remember this
How we danced around each other
Quietly,
Discreetly,
Wordlessly,
No words for joy.
No words for love.
'Ok' a statement,
A pronouncement.
A sealing and ending of arguments,
Never anything really said,
A drifting,
A politeness,
Lies maybe,
Truths nevertheless,
We kept dancing farther away,
Skipping the beats,
Losing the rhythms,
Till there was only a vacant space.

The lilies bloomed beautiful cups.
Now they are withered,
Sun beaten,
Rain drenched,
Not one drop of water had shelter.

They droop,
They fall,
They rot,
They wither,
Our dance a drop of rain on a lily cup.

A Relationship

Unsure, reserved, afraid, scared
Of my secrets, unwilling to share them
Clouded by me and my perceptions,
Sensitive about my issues,
Holding on to my inhibitions,
My hang-ups, my pet peeves
Shy about letting you in,
Into my world, my space, my body.
Contemplating whether this will lead.
To love, to tears, to fulfilment,
Intrigued about you,
Curious about your ideas,
Perplexed, overwhelmed;
Too many thoughts in my head,
All the things you've said have rushed in like a whirlwind,
Rip-rolling, tail-curling, mass stampeding, tree up rooting,
Carrying me on a roller coaster ride.
It's a new thing in my life,
It may be exciting, scary, funny,
Crazy or downright the strangest yet loveliest gift I've ever received.

Unguarded heart

In a room full of people,
    Pulsating loudly,
        The heartbeat races!
Hidden smiles temper strong conversations,
    Coded messages tap on surfaces,
        Embedded in jokes, off color stories.
Responses to no particular questions,
    Timings and impulse chiming together,
        Chords woven in a sensual outlet,
Clues in movement,
    Listening ear through stressful disappointments,
        Silences reverberating with loudness,
Intentions hidden yet seen,
    A heart worn on the sleeve,
        Its fragility heavily guarded,
From onlookers not…
    Directed to its target.
        Freedom a price,
Consciously unpaid,
    Seeing always,
        Feeling unguarded.

Searching

Through magazine pages,
Glued to computer screens,
Viewing reality TV,
Eyeing fantasy through books,
Following friends on social media,
Listening to family gossip,
Searching and searching,

Youth flies on,
Age gains wisdom,
Watching and waiting,
Searching,

The connections fleeting,
The ties do not bind,
Better or for worse,
No promises ascribed,

Games played,
No winners, No losers,
Life's happening!
No Grand celebrations,
Fireworks suspended.

Rescue and find,
Hobbies, clues,
Travels, books,
Dating despite,
Crushes, infatuation,
Fantasies, spiritual retreats,
Concluding acceptance.

The bar set too high or too low.
Love is passion!
Pull it closer,
Set it free like a summer's kite,

Watch and dream!

The end a Revelation.

A flame

Today is the day we decided to hold back,
To close off, to rein in, to control the impulse,
The feeling, the thrill and contain the excitement.

We make polite talk,
We give each other space,
We drown ourselves into work and doldrums,
Passing time: hours, minutes, seconds,
Holding it in.
Such honesty!
We train our feelings to stop,
Our hearts to deny.
Living in the mundane and forgetting,
Erasing, replacing, and curtailing the dream.
Alas deep down in the frail recesses of our hearts,
There is a flicker!
It hides,
Awaiting the day to be fanned aflame again.

A word like love

Love is asking and caring about the response,
It's making sure you're comfortable and warm,
Caressed with warmth through hot beverages when you're sick.
It's making sure you leave home suitably attired and well fed.
It's checking to make sure you have the important things for your journey,
Through checklist that you have covered all your bases.
In days of hurt and injury, disappointments and failure,
It provides a place for sleep and respite, tenderness and hope.
Gathering up your loneliness, bonding through experience.
A word like love is woven in a quilt,
Embroidered in golden moments,
Knitted in scarves,
Sewn in hemlines.
A word like love seeks to find you when you've been exiled,
Traumatized by pain,
Slept in a hard place,
Felt forsaken,
Broken down in tears.
A word like love says, it is well,
Both now and then.
Sending signals connecting through threads spread across oceans and continents,
Heard through codes, messages so clear.
A word like love settles between us,

Transcending through this life and the next.
Repealing sorrow, preserving joy.
Like a family photo on a mantelpiece,
A word like love fades in colors,
The captured moment etched in time.

When I want to kiss you

The Earth stops,
The Moon orbits slowly,
Like an eclipse an overshadowing,
A hushed silence.
A trepidation!

When I want to kiss you,
A fresh smell of a clean snowy day appears,
Like the freshness of spring,
A witnessing,
A calm,
A wistfulness!

When I want to kiss you,
A dream appears,
An apparition like you,
Haunting,
Swift!
Moving through space.

When I want to kiss you,
I close my eyes,
Feel,
Taste,
Breathe you in,
Slowly,

Re-assuredly,
Softly,
With finesse, a gentleness.

When I want to kiss you,
My heart rocks,
Tumbles,
Beats faster,
My pulse quickens,
Heat thickens,
Hands need mittens,
We are smitten.

When I want to kiss you,
The Earth shakes,
An earthquake!
A massive eruption,
Met with contractions.

When I want to kiss you I pause,
I touch,
I see,
I feel you,
Like the mist,
There is a kiss.

A Lover's Heart

A lover's heart
Cares when you're
Sick,
Hurt,
Tired,
Low in mood,
Stressed from life,
Feeling lost.
A lover's heart knows,
When to pull you close,
When to give you space,
When to forgive,
When to wrap up you,
In a swaddling cloth of love.

A lover's heart
Sees and feels,
Your pain and joys,
Hopes and dreams,
And all your fears:
Warm in winter,
Growing in spring,
Playful in summer,
Caressing you through the changing autumn.

A lover's heart,
Sings the tune of your heart,
Dances to the beat of your drum,
And plays the flute of your loins.
A lover's heart weeps for distance's sake,
Hoping to keep you safe.

Out of sync

Incomprehensible.
Behaviors and feelings
Minds and heart,
Do not always align successfully.

Life.
Seeking for understanding,
Hoping words will penetrate the open space,
At the right time,
Healing or wounding with alacrity.

I'm here you're there,
No desire to awaken from the dream,
Sorry to have spoken out of turn
Too soon!
Struggling to keep up;
To hear those words,
Written for you, with you in mind.

Melodies

The lyrics composed,
Fit artfully with the mood,
The banging of the deaf musician,
On chords so well known,
Rhythms superfluous,
Tame and wild,
Bouncing off the instruments.

The crescendo ending in a falsetto,
The bridge of the song a first note,
A New beginning!

A voice ringing out triumphant,
Two beats here.
Two beats there,
Wrapped around violin strings,
Noisy chorus breaks out,
The enthusiastic choir director,
Bustles up in frustrated raptures,
The music floats in unison with rapt voices,
The crescendo dies down,
We float into each other,
A temporary bonding of souls,
Branding the rebels under their camisoles.

Prism of Possibilities

She exists in absentia,
A mist hanging over the morning,
The first dewdrop so sweetly fragrant,
A feeling she has but shuts up with denial.

He exists in expectancy,
A breaking of thunder,
Wrapped up in the first rain of the season.
The showers so big,
People rush to get out of it.
After it breaks the earth is so fresh,
An embodying of newness.

They exist in an open space of dreams,
Between sleeping and waking,
Between the end of the first light of the morning,
And the closing shadows of the evening.

He looks at her with those eyes,
A story she sees but does not see.
A pair of eyes that asks her to look back at him.
A certain touch of vulnerability,
Captured in a glimpse.

She takes stock of everything,
Measuring time backwards,
Conditioning herself to enter into spontaneity,
A flow of choices mingled in a rapid river course.

He paces himself,
Knowing both the choice and the dilemma,
Whispering through spring flowers,
Bringing both pollens and sweet-smelling blossoms.

She looks out the window of life,
Fidgeting for answers,
She hangs up her thoughts.
A crusader of emotions.

Softly she sits down,
Scribbles a few lines,
Centering her passion,
Hanging out her fears to dry.

They waited in an endless cue,
A line up behind work, responsibilities, favors
A chore that was still undone.
They offered a penny in a wishing well,
Arousing Spiritism
Bending the light,
Through a carved prism of possibilities.

Happiness

Happiness is letting yourself forget the pain,
Forgive the past,
Delight in the present,
Sing a song,
Say a prayer,
Accept healing,
Finding your path,
After such a complicated maze.
Believing in yourself,
Trusting in the power of the universe,
Claiming the victory.
Finding yourself on the other side of fear,
Pushing up towards the sunlight,
Sensing some glory moments,
Gravitating towards wholeness,
Grabbing onto life with both hands,
Doing the victory dance,
Knowing your time is now,
A perfect alignment,
Hope's signal of prosperity.
Crossing the threshold,
Beating the odds,
Your spirit coming of age,
Sanctified in your soul,

Resting in calmness,
Thrilled to be alive,
Giving your last coin to the needy,
Earth's provision sufficient to take care of us.
Exercising faith,
Knowing the promises,
The key to happiness.

There is...

There is a place,
A time,
For hearts to sing,
For hearts to dance,
For hearts to advance,
For hearts to retreat,

There is a place for memory,
To standstill,
To recreate,
To recapture,
To relive,

There is a moment,
For choosing now,
For striking hot,
For relinquishing,
For foreboding,

There is an understanding when,
To give up,
To give in,
To give away,
To give back,

There is a feeling,
Of achievement,
Of pride,
Of ruin,
Of victory.

There is the existence when,
Time stops,
Hope freezes,
Control diminishes,
Confusion increases,

For, of, when
There is,
Time, place, feeling and scrutiny.

See you...

See you...
At the crossing,
At the bridge,
At the converging.
See you...
Next when we're both grown into our dreams,
See you...
After you have been broken and healed,
See you...
In movement, in hope, willingness, in art,
See you...
There,
At the closing,
The transitioning of transient people, refugees,
A place, a dialogue, a home.
See you...
On the journey
Where joy sits down and communes with peace.
See you!

Stoplight

A morning,
Overslept,
Running late,
Then it rains,
The bus pulls up jam-packed,
Then it slows to a stop,
A red light,
It lasts for 30 seconds,
A lifetime it seems.
Today I recollect,
You came,
When it rained,
And held me up at a red light,
Then my plans got quietly derailed.

Thrill of the moment

A steamy coupling,
A march on the fixture of furniture,
A time sealed up,
A smell,
A passion,
Only a breath away,

In the thrill of the moment,
With currents running high,
Their touch a flood of electricity,
Like eagles they soared to the sky.

The Quest

Flirting with misguided cues,
The Inevitable in out of sync lines,
A musical key playing notes backwards,
DO, TI, LA, SO, FA, RE DO...
In constant unison,
Played on violins, guitars and mad stomp bands.

A charisma chiming out of tune,
The quest driven and broken, into compounds parts,
Love a foreign concept,
Shapeless!

The boundless overflowing of consummation,
The softness floats,
The glory of it all!

Transitioning

The pain of hearts on fire,
Becoming a shade of something that we can't face,
A monster, like a man trapped in a cold place.
A complicated place to be,
To experience a breakable moment.

A hard place of recovery,
Through streams of consciousness,
A truly long day,
Finding happiness, unsure of accepting it.

Turbulence approaching,
Trying to stay in control,
A place to inadvertently do the right thing.
Chasing rumors and ghosts,

Engineering the journey,
Leaving the unclaimed baggage behind,
Replacing something that has been lost,
Finding closure!

Unity

Hearts united as one,
Thematic, romantic bonds,
In a few stolen moments.

Reflection

Wishing away the corners of you,
    Some time ago,
A day of stoic reflection.

Musing

My thoughts now underscore my feelings,
I absolutely don't know.
Radars picked up mixed signals
Transmission waves faulty.

Keeping busy with my own stuff,
Keeping thoughts of you at arm's length.
Wishing it all away.
I just can't stay in that place where you want me to stay.
I feel stuck
Hang up on you,
Crazy whirly feelings,
Has me spinning in my head.
Something happened!
You pulled away!
After we thought things had settled into a right rhythm.

Musings with a cup of tea,
Helps to refine the thesis question.
Men changing tune when women chase them.
Instead of me trying to know,
Let it go!
You only win when he surrenders to your surrender to him.

I Want Your Life

Two women share thoughts over a cup of coffee.
'I want your life' she said.
Freedom to travel,
Visiting exotic places,
Exploring enchanting cultures,
Gratifying expanding taste buds,
Throwing caution to the wind,
Eschewing your own choices,
No one to vet your decisions,
A wide open port of portals,
To transfer you forward,
Charting your own destiny,
No grave commitment to tie you down,
Or responsibility to hedge you in.
"I want your life", she declares.

"Do you really?" The other friend said.
My life in pictures shows you,
The polished moments.
The beautiful backgrounds,
The grandeur of experiencing new things,
On the surface so captivating,
Underneath I'm breaking,
Skating on thin ice,
Seldom escaping unscathed.
Having many acquaintances,

Lacking deep friendships,
Set on fast forward,
Moving always to escape the loneliness,
The depression that tries to consume me.
I've lost love,
I had my heart broken in so many places.
Yet became the envy of so many people.
Broken down in tears, fell flat on my face,
Experienced the hospital of life,
Where no one comes to visit you.
Felt the twisted writhing pain,
Crashed on my bathroom floor,
Sick and all alone.

My life appearing glamorous,
Money able to sign a contract with happiness,
Lacking in fulfillment and worthiness,
Craving the simple things of life,
A house with a family to in dwell,
Cooking three meals a day,
Washing, scrubbing, cleaning,
Wiping noses, arranging play and recreation.
Standing in collective mess,
Accepting the natural course of life,
Blessed be the ties that bind.
School run and after school activities,
Birthdays and play dates,
Cuddling on a sofa to watch the rerun of a movie.
Voices in the house, laughter at the dinner table,
Petty squabbles and play fighting,
Bunching us together against the world.

My life in value cannot compare,
A floating emptiness sits near.

"You want my life", she said to her friend.
"No, you can't imagine it.
I'd be happy to have your life."

Sometimes I'm a Poet

Sometimes I'm a poet,
Caught in the stillness of nature,
Thinking about dreams,
Seeing bloom and decay.
Feeling hearts that hurt,
Wounds that never heal.
Caught in sadness,
My eyes saw all kinds of petals,
Colorful and beautiful.
A brief occasion to smile.
A warmth hugging the soul.

Peace

Seeing the clouds as they lifted from the room,
True thoughts hanging on a rainbow in the sky,
Hanging out to dry.
No weaved in illusions or undertones of disdain,
Suspended in hot air balloons,
Coming back to earth.
Forgiveness laid on a quilt of blessings,
Smiling and walking away,
In stillness.
Peace be yours!

"Overtime our hearts become engaged with those around us, whether we set out to do so or not. Saying goodbye is not only about leaving from each other, but also the understanding that our encounters will no longer be intertwined. Our moments of sharing thoughts, ideas and friendship maybe diminished forever!"

(Written in response to friends leaving Japan at the end of their work contract- February, 2009).

> "Every journey brings us new encounters and every encounter brings us new discoveries" (Written in a note to a friend leaving China, July 2015)

PHOTOS

ENCOUNTERS WITH OTHER CULTURES

My Japanese Maiko experience,
Beauty and tradition extrapolate and intertwine.

Kokoro-Heart
Writing my kanji my heart swells.

A glimpse of a rare Amami island bird.
Capturing moments through a camera lens.

Amami Oshima tsumugi – A treasured art in fabric and style.

Visiting Xi'an,
The ancient warriors to see,
Absorbing a bite size of the history,
Feeling the pulse of the city.
Chinese traditional opera.

Hanfu and Tea Culture a charming time spent,
Fellow students of Chinese language and culture,
Meet to consider and celebrate!
(Chinese style traditional clothing courtesy of Emma Chen.
Pictures courtesy of Chinese Surfing Language School) Date
taken: November 28. 2020.

Index

Encounters with places

Japan for J.E.T.S 11
My travels 13
The Grand Canal 16
Uneven pavements 17
Navigating Ruins 19
Convergence 20
Landscape 1: 21
Landscape 2: 22
Landscape 3: 23

Encounters with a myriad of feelings

Half- Wit 27
Left to Chance 28
Transient Roles 29
Mellowing 30
Seeds 32
Beginning and End 33
Precedence 34
Seasons of You 36
Detaching 38

Encounters 39
Standing in a standstill 40
Hearts near a wishing well 42
The Hammer.. 43
What is Love? 44
Romance with Words 45
Symmetry 47

Encounters with spiritual/ positive light

Buds Opening 51
First of June 52
Life 53
I am a woman rising 54

Encounter with love and loss

Lily Cups 57
A Relationship 59
Unguarded heart 60
Searching 61
A flame.. 63
A word like love.. 64
When I want to kiss you... 66
A Lover's Heart 68
Out of sync 70
Melodies 71
Prism of Possibilities 72
Happiness.. 74

There is…	76
See you…	78
Stoplight	79
Thrill of the moment	80
The Quest	81
Transitioning	82
Unity	83
Reflection	84
Musing	85
I Want Your Life	86
Sometimes I'm a Poet	89
Peace	90
Photos	92

www.ingramcontent.com/pod-product-compliance
Lightning Source LLC
Chambersburg PA
CBHW052212090526

44584CB00019BA/3054